DOGS TO THE RESCUE!

WILDERNESS SEARCH DOGS

By Sara Green

BELLWETHER MEDIA • MINNEAPOLIS, MN

Jump into the cockpit and take flight with Pilot books. Your journey will take you on high-energy adventures as you learn about all that is wild, weird, fascinating, and fun!

This edition first published in 2014 by Bellwether Media, Inc.

No part of this publication may be reproduced in whole or in part without written permission of the publisher. For information regarding permission, write to Bellwether Media, Inc., Attention: Permissions Department, 5357 Penn Avenue South, Minneapolis, MN 55419.

Library of Congress Cataloging-in-Publication Data

Green, Sara, 1964-
  Wilderness search dogs / by Sara Green.
    pages cm. – (Pilot. Dogs to the rescue!)
  Includes bibliographical references and index.
  Summary: "Engaging images accompany information about wilderness search dogs. The combination of high-interest subject matter and narrative text is intended for students in grades 3 through 7"– Provided by publisher.
  ISBN 978-1-60014-962-7 (hardcover : alk. paper)
  1. Search dogs–Juvenile literature. I. Title.
  SF428.73.G738 2014
  636.7'0886–dc23
                                                    2013014519

Printed in the United States of America, North Mankato, MN.

TABLE OF CONTENTS

A DOG TO THE RESCUE!

Three hikers wander off a trail in the **wilderness**. They think they know a shortcut back to their car. As they walk, the **terrain** becomes steep and rocky. The hikers do not recognize any **landmarks**. They are lost. Suddenly, one of the hikers trips on a sharp rock. She hurts her leg and cannot walk. Darkness sets in. The hikers are cold, scared, and in need of help.

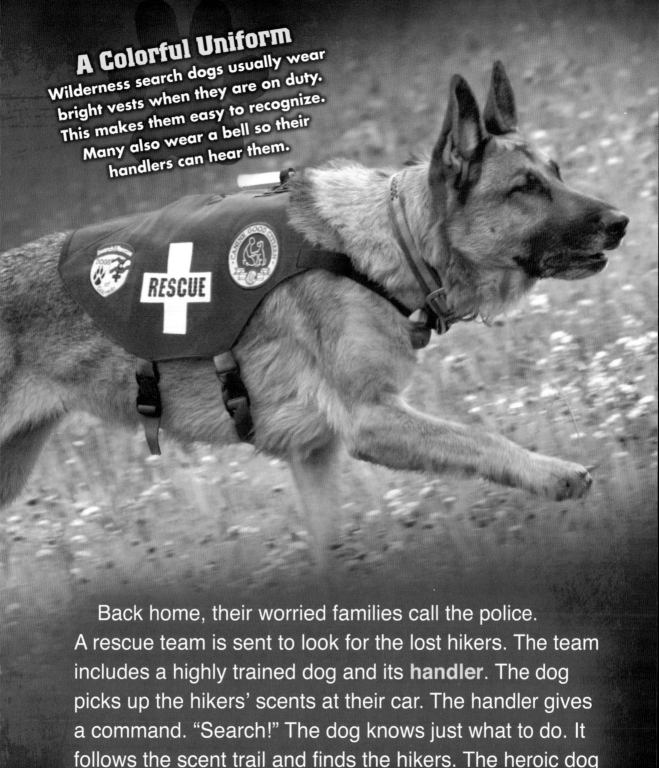

A Colorful Uniform

Wilderness search dogs usually wear bright vests when they are on duty. This makes them easy to recognize. Many also wear a bell so their handlers can hear them.

RESCUE

Back home, their worried families call the police. A rescue team is sent to look for the lost hikers. The team includes a highly trained dog and its **handler**. The dog picks up the hikers' scents at their car. The handler gives a command. "Search!" The dog knows just what to do. It follows the scent trail and finds the hikers. The heroic dog saves the day!

WHAT IS A WILDERNESS SEARCH DOG?

Wilderness search dogs use their keen sense of smell to find people lost in wilderness areas. Dogs have very sensitive noses. They can find people faster than humans can. These specially trained dogs search for people in forests, mountains, and deserts. They also search in fields, parks, and the edges of towns.

The dogs and their handlers work day and night during a rescue **mission**. They work in all kinds of weather and in almost any kind of terrain. They must be able to navigate streams, fallen trees, thick brush, and other obstacles. Some may have to **rappel** down cliffs or crawl into tight spaces. Being a wilderness search dog is tough work!

Dropping In

Many wilderness search dogs are trained to ride in and rappel from helicopters. This way they can quickly get to areas that may be far from roads.

Profile: German Shepherd

Intelligence
The German Shepherd is the third smartest dog breed. The dog will obey new commands almost immediately.

Size
Height: 22 to 26 inches
(56 to 66 centimeters)

Weight: 50 to 95 pounds
(23 to 43 kilograms)

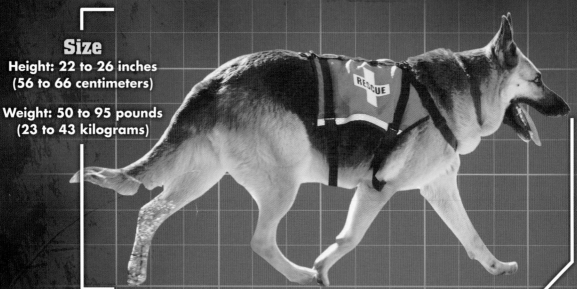

Sensitive Nose
A dog can detect a teaspoon of sugar in a million gallons of water. This is equal to two Olympic-sized swimming pools.

A variety of breeds are used as wilderness search dogs. These include Border Collies, Labrador Retrievers, Golden Retrievers, and German Shepherds. Mixed breeds also make great wilderness search dogs. Many are rescued from shelters. Wilderness search dogs must have strength and **stamina**. They must be intelligent and loyal to their handlers. They must be friendly with both people and other dogs. Wilderness search dogs must also love to play. Searching for people is like a game. Dogs with a strong urge to play often make the best searchers.

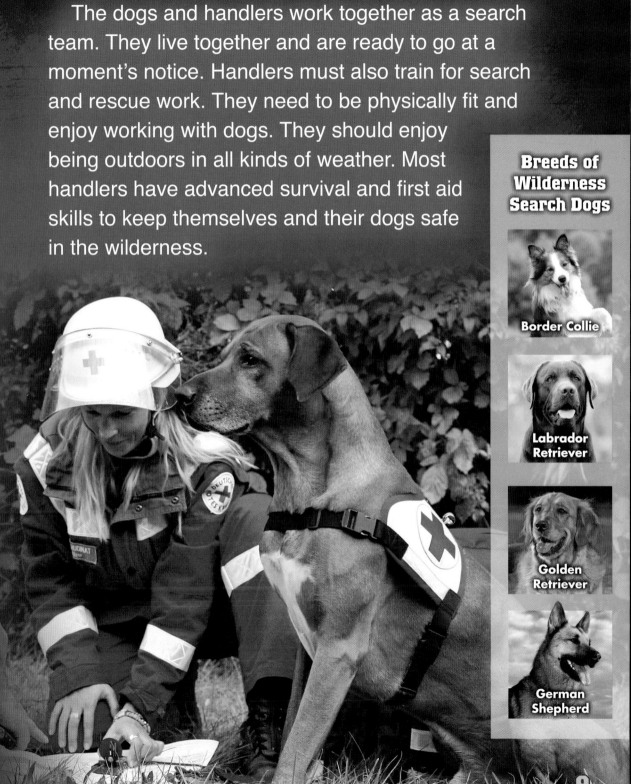

The dogs and handlers work together as a search team. They live together and are ready to go at a moment's notice. Handlers must also train for search and rescue work. They need to be physically fit and enjoy working with dogs. They should enjoy being outdoors in all kinds of weather. Most handlers have advanced survival and first aid skills to keep themselves and their dogs safe in the wilderness.

Breeds of Wilderness Search Dogs

Border Collie

Labrador Retriever

Golden Retriever

German Shepherd

TRAINING FOR DUTY

Most wilderness search dogs train for one to two years before they go on duty. Training often begins when the dogs are puppies. First, they are taught basic **obedience skills** and good manners. They learn to pay attention to the handler and ignore animals, loud noises, food, and other distractions. They become comfortable around strangers and other dogs. The dogs also learn **agility skills**. These include crawling through tunnels, climbing ladders, and walking on narrow beams. The dogs become strong and confident during this training.

The dogs also learn to find strangers. At first, the dogs find strangers who are easy to spot. Next, the dogs find them hiding in fields or behind rocks and trees. When the dogs find the strangers, they receive praise, treats, and playtime. They learn that finding strangers is fun!

After dogs master these basic skills, they are ready to learn advanced search methods. Wilderness search dogs are usually trained to air scent. In this method, dogs sniff the air for the scent of humans. They do not sniff for a particular person. Instead, they sniff the air for the general human scent. As people walk, they shed flakes of dead skin. Large flakes fall to the ground, while small ones drift in the air. These flakes have a scent that dogs can smell.

The wind can carry the human scent long distances. This allows air scenting dogs to search large areas with their noses. People never stop giving off a scent. The dogs can pick up the human scent no matter how much time has passed.

Many Dogs, Many Teams
There are over 150 air scenting dog teams in the United States.

Air scenting dogs work off leash and run in a zigzag pattern. They can explore large areas in a short amount of time. As the dog gets closer to the lost person, the human scent gets stronger. Finally, the dog narrows in on the person and barks to alert the handler. The handler goes to the dog's location to find the lost person.

A World Record Sniff

An air scenting dog in Alaska detected a human from 2 miles (3.2 kilometers) away. This is the longest distance on record.

Many dogs are also trained to **refind**. The dogs locate the lost person, return to their handlers, and lead them back to the person. The dogs always receive rewards for finding people. This means a lot of praise and playtime with the handler!

Many wilderness search dogs are trained to **trail** lost people. They follow a specific person's scent on the ground and on **vegetation**. Trailing dogs begin their search at the last place a person was seen. The dogs sniff a **scent article** that belongs to the lost person. This helps them know what scent to follow. The handler holds the dog's leash as they follow the scent trail together. Trailing dogs must work more quickly than air scenting dogs. A person's scent on the ground gets weaker over time. Other scents cover it. People and animals kick it away. Trailing dogs must begin to search while the lost person's scent is still strong.

After they complete all of their training, the dogs and their handlers receive **certification**. Now they are ready for duty! Wilderness search dogs continue to practice with their handlers every week to keep their skills sharp. Most teams must pass search and rescue tests every two years.

ON A MISSION

At the search scene, the team must be prepared to work hard. They often work 8 to 10 hours a day in stressful conditions. Some missions last two or more days. Search operations may only have a few rescue workers. Others are larger. For these, rescue workers often set up a **base camp**. The base camp is often brightly lit, crowded, and noisy. Police officers may use **bullhorns** to give instructions to rescue workers and family members.

At base camp, the handlers study maps. They divide the search area into sections. Each canine team is responsible for searching one section. Handlers load backpacks with food, water, extra clothes, a first aid kit, and other supplies. This gear includes supplies that dogs and the lost person may need. Handlers always carry radios or walkie-talkies to communicate with rescue workers waiting at base camp. As soon as a dog gives an alert, everyone moves quickly to rescue the lost person.

SOOT: THE WILDERNESS SEARCH DOG

A black Labrador Retriever named Soot is a hero. In 2012, he was named Search and Rescue Dog of the Year by the American Humane Association. Soot lives in West Virginia with his handler, Lorrie Burdette.

One autumn day, Lorrie and Soot got a call. A hunter was lost in the mountains of West Virginia. Lorrie and Soot went to the hunter's truck. There, Soot picked up the hunter's scent. Lorrie and Soot searched for hours. They could not find the hunter. Was he lost for good?

Then someone noticed boot prints farther up the mountain. Lorrie and Soot hurried to the spot. Soot caught the hunter's scent and followed the trail. Finally, he found the hunter. The hunter was very relieved to see Soot. Thanks to this brave dog, the hunter returned home tired but safe.

GLOSSARY

agility skills—skills that involve navigating around obstacles

base camp—a place where people gather to organize a search

bullhorns—devices that make voices louder so they can be heard at a distance

certification—the process that recognizes that a dog has mastered specific job skills

handler—a person who is responsible for a highly trained dog

landmarks—objects or features that help people know where they are

mission—an organized search effort

obedience skills—skills such as sit, stay, down, and come

rappel—to go down a rock face using a rope

refind—to lead a handler back to a person

scent article—an article that a person has touched; a dog smells it to learn the scent of the person.

stamina—the ability to do something for a long time

terrain—a stretch of land

trail—to follow a person's scent left on the ground

vegetation—plants

wilderness—undeveloped land that is home to plants and animals

TO LEARN MORE

AT THE LIBRARY

Bozzo, Linda. *Search and Rescue Dog Heroes*. Berkeley Heights, N.J.: Enslow Publishers, 2011.

Greenberg, Daniel. *Wilderness Search Dogs*. New York, N.Y.: Bearport Publishing, 2005.

Rajczak, Kristen. *Rescue Dogs*. New York, N.Y.: Gareth Stevens Publishing, 2011.

ON THE WEB

Learning more about wilderness search dogs is as easy as 1, 2, 3.

1. Go to www.factsurfer.com.

2. Enter "wilderness search dogs" into the search box.

3. Click the "Surf" button and you will see a list of related Web sites.

With factsurfer.com, finding more information is just a click away.

INDEX